Become

How to be the person you most admire

MIGUEL WILLIAMS

Become:
How to be the person you most admire

To order more copies for you or your team, go to
www.miguelwilliams.com

Discover what kind of world you want to live in,
Accept nothing less than that from yourself or anyone around you.

Table Of Content

Introduction

The difficulty of the task is exactly why you should do it.

For as long as we can remember, we've all had dreams, wishes, desires, goals, wants, many we've achieved and even more, we haven't. The majority of us find ourselves with a long list of unfulfilled achievements, which overwhelms the enjoyment of our lives.

Participants of a scientific study were asked, to name their single biggest life regret, 76 per cent cited an action they did not take that would have helped them realise their ideal self. The number one reason people do not take these potentially life-changing actions is, fear.

We all want to be smarter, financially stable and live a healthy, happy, fulfilled lifestyle, yet, we struggle to achieve all or any of these desires over our entire lifetime. Think about it, a lifetime of dreams, wishes, desires and goals unaccomplished, this is the life billions of people are living today. They are settling for the life they have instead of going after the life they dream of living.

You've landed in the right place, this is not a self-help, personal development book, look at this as a toolbox, here, you will be given the tools to become a super achiever.

This book is written for the person who is seeking to evolve themselves into an Extra Mile being, (someone who desires, plans and takes action on an extraordinary level most don't know exist).

You will not acquire supernatural powers but you will gain superior insight, understanding and philosophies, to achieve any desired goals. I will show you how to become the person you admire most in the world, how to dominate your life, create and control the tools you need to achieve the goals you set yourself. How to reach your full potential and eliminate any limiting forces holding you back. By the end of our journey, you should graduate, a better thinker, strategist and action taker. There should be no limits on what you can achieve.

My Story,
Getting Off The Sofa.

You cannot change your destination overnight,
but you can change your direction overnight.
-Jim Rohn-

It was December 28, 2015, my birthday, my eyes slowly opened to the bright daylight blasting through the window, I felt horrible, my back ached, I was uncomfortable and unhappy. I was sleeping on my mother's sofa. I did not crash or made a bad sleeping choice the night before, this was my bed, where I've slept every night for months, this was my life. She was kind enough to let me stay here, as all good parents would but most probably, not proudly.

I made some unwise past decisions, resulting in me being a 30-year-old squatter on my mother's sofa, with nothing to show for all my years on earth. I felt disappointed in myself but I did not know my family might have been as well. I was talking to my younger brother, attempting to give him some big brotherly life advice when he replied, "Look at your situation," and he was right. Look at my situation, and I did, I looked. How could he confidently take my advice about his life, when mine was nothing for him to aspire to, he could not look up to me or follow in my footsteps, and I did not blame him.

My Brother's comment sat with me, I started looking at my life, and surely I did not like what I was seeing, this is embarrassing. I kept asking myself, what the hell happened? how did I let this happen to me? How did I end up here? I made a decision that I will not live like this anymore. I started to analyse my life and how I made decisions. I came across the teachings of Jim Rohn, the American author and speaker, his philosophies on personal development changed everything for me. Exploring business philosophies, I studied the work of Jay Abraham, a master business strategist, both teachers have become heroes of mine, their lessons in both life and business have served me beyond my wildest dreams. I learned to become a student of my past and the architect of my future.

In search of further growth, I seek the mentorship of successful people I admired and studied them diligently. I changed, I grow, my fortunes started to improve, I was now happy and proud of the life I was living and the future to come.

Looking around, I realised there were many people stuck in the situation I was once in, I wanted to help them take back control of their lives. I became a consultant, helping small businesses and entrepreneurs scale and realise their dreams. I am still en route to my desired destination and I want to help others realise their dreams along the way.

The Story
That Drives You

This book is for you and about you, who you were, who you are and who you wish to become. So, what is your story? What have you been doing with your life so far? Are you where you want to be or have you fallen off course? Have you given up control of your life to the forces of nature, screaming, forget it! let whatever happens, happen, I will just see how life goes?

If this is or was you, then we are about to embark on a journey together. Let me show you how I got out of that place and strived, beyond my greatest imagination. They say the mine is only limited to what we allow it to believe, so I employ you to truly set your mind free, let it sore beyond what you can contemplate at the moment, you will catch up to it one day.

The Past

Let's start with why you are the person you are today, living the life you are living, at the destination you are right now. Think back five years ago, is the life you are living now what you had planned back then?

Our past choices and actions are a direct result of the present life we are living, so, that means, our present choices and actions will be a direct result of the future life we will live. I urge you to stop and take stock of your present life. If you are not were to want to be now, then I suggest you not repeat your past actions in the present, we can all agree they are not the correct actions to help you achieve the future life you desire.

We all wish we could go back and change things from our past, since that is not an option we should try to reflect on the past, to learn how we can make better decisions next time around. There are two pieces of gold to bring from your past, what you did wrong and what you did right, then explore how you did them, what motivated you and how you felt after. Whilst what you did wrong will tell you what mistakes not to repeat, what you did right should serve as your guide on how to approach future problems and projects. Reflecting on our accomplishments brings back, encouraging, positive and creative drives, energising us with confidence. Do you remember passing your driving test, graduating from college, passing your exams, getting your dream job, landing that first client, getting that first date? Recall on these past accomplishments to boost your energy for the present. You have accomplished so much already, draw strength from your past wins to fuel your present challenges, if you have done it once you can do it again.

Failure is our greatest teacher, failure when used correctly can propel you to incredible achievements. Failure is only accomplished when you give up on the goals you are trying to achieve, when you do not use your mistakes to learn and make better future decisions. Your future can be much more successful than your past and present life if utilise the lessons of your past.

We should use the past as a school to learn from our failures and mistakes, not an anchor to dwell on. Take the past knowledge gained in both wins and losses, and apply it forward, to set yourself free to soar onwards into your better future.

The Present and Future

The present is already here, you can no longer prepare for it, you can only experience it.

Your present life experience depends on how well it was designed for you, by you, in the past. If your present life experience is great, then well done, high five and fist bump to your past self for doing a splendid job. If not, then we have some work to do, not to correct the presents, it's too late for that but we can design a better future to later enjoy.

We will be looking at long-term goals through this book because I want to encourage you to become a big-picture thinker. I want you to embrace the big picture, every truly successful person has a grand big-picture vision for their life and since you are here to become a truly successful person, then I hope you too will become a big-picture visionary.

Here is some very good news, you have been to school and graduated a decision-making expert (via your past mistakes and achievements). Whilst you will still make mistakes and fail, *embrace it* (I call failures and mistakes learning) you are equipped with a wealth of past failures and mistakes to make better decisions to live a more prosperous present and to design and build the successful future you desire.

Let's get to work immediately, by cutting out the things that are preventing you from achieving a better life and implementing more of the things that will help you strive and enjoy the extraordinary life you desire.

You are amazing! Yes, I said it, and I mean it, and you deserve to enjoy the best life has to offer. Remember the last vacation or special event you enjoyed with your friends, family, or just that special someone? It did not just happen, you planned it, weeks, months, years in advance. In the past, you worked overtime, saved and made sacrifices so that you could one day in the future enjoy that vacation - remember how that felt on the day, all the pain and sacrifices you went through was all worth it.

Actions not driving you towards your goals,
are driving you away from achieving them.

Everything you do defines who you are, it is not only the big things, the little unnoticed actions also adds up. Like the butterfly effect, everything affects everything else.

To design the future of your dreams requires you to take, productive, effective, actions now, if each action is not working towards achieving your goal then it should be stopped immediately without hesitation. You will have to learn to cut down on the bad stuff, like, too much TV, Facebook, Youtube surfing, weekend night outs, hanging around negative non-ambitious people.

You must ensure that everything you do is directly connected to making your future life a better experience. This will leave you more time to meet, like-minded, creative, ambitious people, to network, be inspired by and partner with. You will be more in tune and energised by your future, you will not want to go back to TV binging or falling out of a cab drunk at 4 am. Let me stress, there are many ways to have fun and spend your downtime to destress, I encourage downtime but how you do it and with whom is also very important, surround yourself with successful, positive, driven people at all times, they are who you will become.

Now is the perfect time. Why now? Because right now is the best time ever, for you to take the actions needed to make your future a pleasant experience. Remember that you will have to live this life tomorrow, the day after and all the other days and nights to come, death is your only escape, so ensure the actions you take now, are ones which will help enhance your future experiences.

Live In The Present, Work In The Future.

"Look after today, tomorrow will take care of itself". I do not recommend this approach to life. I hope I have made this very clear, you should not be working on your present life in the present, you should be living and experiencing your present life because it was already designed and prepared for you in the past.

While you are living and enjoying this amazing present life, design and create a better life experience for your future self to later enjoy. Unforeseen circumstances will accrue and should be dealt with accordingly but never the less, what you can influence, make it your duty to do so. Develop this approach today and you will start to look towards your future with a smile of anticipation and excitement.

The Story That Drivers Your Desires

I have a sweet little question for you, why are you pursuing the career path you are on now?

I am an entrepreneur at heart but I understand it is not everyone's calling, some people like the security of a job and that is absolutely perfect for them, we are all different and therefore will not see life the same - and that is fine. Whatever path you choose to walk, what drives you as an entrepreneur, an artist or an employee?

My mission is to *Help People Live Better Lives*, sure, I could achieve this goal via many other paths. I found that when I embarked on my journey and I needed help with my life, I was only successful because of the teachings of others, the mentors I encountered. I want to be an extension of the people who helped me improve my life, by helping others improve theirs. I find great satisfaction in helping others enjoy the best life they can and fulfilling their dreams.

You too have your own story, why do you want to start a family? Why do you want to pick your family up and move to another country to pursue a career? Why do you want to work at the new startup for less than you currently earn in an already established organisation? Whatever endeavours you wish to pursue, find your why, find your story. Your story will give you sticking power to call on for energy and motivation when adversity challenges your mission. Too often people abandon their dreams because they are not clear on why they pursued them in the first place.

Greatness Is On The Top Shelf

This is not an intervention, however, in order to reach higher and achieve greatness we have to grow, our philosophy has to change. Let's cut to it, you are aspiring to achieve something new, there are skills, knowledge and disciplines you have not yet possess, therefore, you have not yet become the person that will achieve these desires and be able to live prosperously with them. Simply put, you cannot achieve anything, you do not yet have the skills to achieve. You cannot paint a masterpiece until you learn and acquire the skills of a masterful painter.

The great thing about skills are, they are not assigned at birth and if you did not get the one you wanted you were out of luck. Skills are teachable, they can be learnt. Michael Jordan learnt the skills required to play like he did, Messi and Ronaldo learnt the skills needed to play like they do, Serena Williams learnt the skills to play like she does. Name them all, if you are privileged to see behind the scenes of their lives, the greats you admire are all hard at practice on their skills. Personal Development is practice, I employ you to start training at once.

Becoming The Person Of Your Dreams

This is an incredible exercise I learnt from Warren Buffett. The power of modelling other people is a terrific time leveraging tool, in both business and personal development.

Grab a notebook and write down the names of five people you admire and want to be like, they can be anyone, even TV or book characters. Then, for each person, write five reasons why you admire them.

Also, write the names of five people you do not admire and do not want to be like, and write five reasons why not for each person.

Now, this will take some heart but it will be worth it. Do the same for yourself, write your name in full - make it real. Write five things you admire about yourself, then, five things you do not admire about yourself.

Now, under the heading, Do More Of These, write the list of things you admire about the people you've chosen and yourself.

Then, under the heading, Work On These, write the list of things you do not admire about the people you've chosen and yourself.

Keep both lists side-by-side where you can see them every day. Now you will see the person you are working to become and the person you are working not to become at the same time, these go hand-in-hand and cannot be separated. If every action is not leading you towards becoming the person you want to be, it is driving you to become someone you do not want to be - do not allow this.

With each admiration on your list, what skills do you have to work on to ensure you become more of who you admire?

And, what skills do you have to work on to ensure you do not become who you do not admire?

Before you can achieve and sustained anything, successfully, you have to evolve into a new higher version of yourself. Do not shy away from growing, it is your path to evolution. Wake up every day, knowing, feeling and being happy that you are exactly the person you admire and want to be.

Motivation

Why? For love, money, a better life, your family, fear, faith etc. Everything is done for a reason. They might not be good but there is a reason nevertheless.

Sync with your story, why is a powerful motivator, and your why is what drives everything you have ever achieved, think back to some of the most difficult achievements you've successfully completed. What was the main burning desire that made you not give up when difficulties struck, why exactly did you not give up?

It is the end of another long busy working day, while everyone is excitedly packing away to leave the office, John is settled in, still determinedly working away, he wants to squeeze more from the day. Kate shouts at him, "John, come on, we are heading to the pub for a drink," John replies. "I'll give it a miss, I still have work to do". Now, John has never stayed back after work a day in his life, he was always the last to start in the morning and the first to leave in the evening. Kate is surprised, She enquiries, "This is not like you John, you even being here this late is a shock in itself," John replies, "My wife is pregnant". Motivation can come in many forms, it is something that plucks us out of the drift we once lived comfortably in and fill us with the drive we never knew lived inside us.

It is said that motivation comes from either adversity or desperation. In John's case, it seems desperation of some nature awoke his motivation, he suddenly has a child to care for and support, which became his calling to buckle down and get serious with his work, if he keeps at it, without doubt, he should be able to adequately provide for his new family.

The Power Of Goal Setting

Use your why, to do one of the most powerful things you will ever do for your life in any area, Set Goals. Goals are nature's mystical, unexplainable wizardry, without goals to move towards, something to drive us to achieve, we will drift in the grand ocean of life, blown around and battered by the winds, the waves, and at some point washed up on a shore we do not want to be, like me at 30 years old.

Write Goals > Make Plan > Do Work > Get Results

Not every force can be explained, no one knows why writing down a goal stands a better chance of succeeding than unwritten goals. For as long as I can remember I wanted to be a business owner. I remember, as a child, watching the American soap opera 'The Young And The Restless', my favourite character was Victor Newman, the powerful wealth business owner. I grew up very poor and surprisingly, to my recollection, being wealthy was not what attracted me to the character, he was probably the oldest guy in the show and I was about 9 years old. What really attracted me to want to be like Victor Newman, the businessman, was the freedom and power he seemed to have over his own life. I wanted that freedom and control over my own life and to choose how I would live it.

I always told people I wanted to own a business, it was always my path, when I discovered the power of writing down goals, I wrote that I wanted to become a successful business owner and acquire true freedom over my life, freedom was why. I wrote it daily, spoke it daily and prayed for it daily. I now own an investment company, inspired by my desire for freedom, I named the company Live Free. Embrace the power of goal setting, it is a natural and reliable force.

Don't keep goals in your head, Write Them Down.
Write Them Down. Write Them Down.

"How did I get here?" She asks her Life "I did not ask to be taken here, I do not want to be here". Her Life replies, "Well, you gave me no directions, no destination to take you, you were asleep at the wheels of your Ship, Captain," She questions Her Life, "But why here?" Her Life replies, "Hey, I am your life, it is your duty to plan and drive me in the direction you want me to go, if you cannot be bothered to do that then we will just end up wherever we end up".

Like a Captain setting course to navigate the oceans set your goals, and set them clearly, defined and review them regularly to ensure your grand ship is bang on course to your desired destination and nowhere else. If you find it drifting off the path, do not permit it, make the corrections immediately to bring it back on course.

Seek Knowledge

On your journey you will face resistance, you will be challenged, the storms will attack, battering your ship, the tides will push you around to knock you off course, the wind will rip your sails, to stop you helpless in the middle of the wild ocean. These are not personal attacks on you, just nature at work, everyone faces this brutal voyage in life. Seek the knowledge of those who have journeyed, SUCCESSFULLY, these paths and these conditions before you. They will save you time, energy, cost and could be the difference between you succeeding or completely failing to reach your destination.

Be sure to seek knowledge from the ones who HAVE journeyed the path or are accomplished and proven experts in what you seek to learn. Like the infamous fake news, fake knowledge is also a trend. Knowledge is a treasure but the wrong knowledge is like splashing out a fortune on what you think was a sparkling piece of diamond that turns out to be useless glass. Filter the advice you receive at all times, it might come from someone with good intentions, however, it is your duty to ensure you test the information you receive.

When you do find the knowledge you seek, and it is tested to be the real deal become a diligent student, do not be lazy in learning - absorb everything that is available, leave nothing on the table.

Do not be cheap when paying for knowledge, I am not saying to take out a loan and get the most expensive designer stuff on the market, when shopping for knowledge the value you pay, in both money and time, should give you infinite return on your investment. Say you paid for and took an accounting class, how long should that new accounting skill last you?... Forever? Yes!

If you learned to Tango, you might not be able to physically bust those moves at age 90 but you will still know how to.

Let me point out that you will not and should not attempt to know it all. Yes, continue the art and science of personal development and continuous learning but stick to developing the passions and skills you want to learn and use. There are plenty of people both passionate and skilled in the areas you have no interest in but you will require those skills to succeed, find these people, partner with or hire them and give them the tasks you have no interest in, they do, so they will be glad to do them for you - this process is called Delegating, learn it and use it with pride.

Assemble Your Avengers

The people we surround ourselves with, heavily reflect the life we live. They go further than just reflect it, they also affect our level of success. There are no successful billionaires spending days of the week hanging out with unemployed broke friends, they don't even have them. When shopping (yes shopping, because you are choosing them) for the right people to spend your time with, those who will help you move in the direction of your goals and greatly enhance your ability to achieve them, you need to ensure they are right for you. You have to audition the people you give your time and ensure they are adding positive, productive value to your life. Look at your friends and family and ask yourself the below questions.

Here is a checklist:

1. Who do I spend my time with?
2. What are they doing to me?
3. Is this association ok with me?

Look at each person you spend major time with:
1. Is it positive and constructive or is it negative and destructive?
2. Are my present associations with this person helping me grow in the direction of the goals I have chosen to achieve?

It is not an easy task to cut people you care about from your life but if you cannot make the difficult decisions to better your life, you will never have the life you truly desire.

Successful people follow this process, they only associate with people who are right for them. Copy the philosophies of successful people, if they have a magic formula that has been tested and it works very well, use it, do not recreate the wheel, the one that works, works, just use it.

Becoming
More Valuable

Life does not give you what you want, life gives you what you deserve.
- Jim Rohn -

To become better, you have to become more valuable to your marketplace - where you wish to earn more for the services you render. This applies to all areas of your life, to increase your value, you should read the required books, take the necessary classes, seek mentorship from leaders on the subjects you wish to masters, attend the seminars and buy the courses to improve your knowledge. Do not be cheap in acquiring the knowledge you seek and do not be lazy in learning. If you must do one thing in life forever, it is continuing to learn, improve and increase in value.

Become a better husband, wife, parent, brother, sister, friend.

Become a better leader, employee, listener, speaker, member of the community.

Become a better ... (anything you value and want to participate in).

Put all you have, in all you do, to receive the best from yourself.

Have you ever wondered why you get paid a few thousand dollars a year and someone else gets paid millions for the same year's work? We all get the same 365 days, yet some people cash-in a few thousand and others get paid millions or even billions per year. If you look at the Forbes rich list, it is amazing what people are getting paid compared to you and me. Why is that? Because, we all get paid according to the value of our output, in the marketplace.

If in your job, you bring in one million dollars of income for the company you work in and you get 10% of that total revenue, you will earn yourself 100 thousand dollars. However, if you anchor down, gain more knowledge and skills in your field and really poured it on next year, then earned the company ten million dollars, your 10% cut will now be a sweet one million dollars. That is the same 365 days but you got paid 10x the amount of money to do the same job in the same amount of time. You were not promoted, all you did was increase yourself in value, then to your market, by earning more money in the same amount of time.

Becoming more valuable does not mean you have to increase your workload, it simply means you increase your skills, knowledge and capabilities, which will allow you to take on and execute larger tasks, with better success rates. Why do some football players on the same team get paid 2-3-4-5 times more than their teammates? Because they are more valuable to the club, they are much better players, and perhaps have a better off-pitch market value (celebrity), which brings in more merchandise revenues, ticket sales and higher purchase price by another team.

Invincible, Unshakable, Success

Life gives you a lossy result, when you give it a lossy effort.

Success is a desire of many faces, it means different things to different people. A poor husband might label his life successful because he has a happy marriage. A rich wife might label her life successful because she is a self-made millionaire. Whatever face success wears in your life, when you achieve it celebrate and relish in it because very few get to realise their life goals.

The feeling of success, when acquired, brings a distinct feeling of pride, accomplishment, status, genius, prosperity, superiority, freedom and leadership. Achieving success gives a person elevated empowerment in themselves that makes them feel better about who they are and what they can accomplish from their life. The reason why successful people keep on achieving more and more success is due to what I call, The Success Snowball Effect. One small success validates a person's abilities which empowers them to take on a bigger challenge, the success of the bigger challenge then heightens their validation and creates greater empowerment, which invites even bigger challenges to aspire to, and this process is repeated.

On the other hand, if a person does not feel successful, even if they just failed a simple driving test, they can feel distorted, unworthy, invaluable, dull and foolish, as if they are average and at the bottom of the world's ladder. If you keep trying until you succeed, your confidence will be at such a superior level you will not drift into despair because of a few failures. Your list of failures should always be longer than your success list, if you study some of the most successful people in the world they have failed more times than they have succeeded. Thomas Edison failed over one thousand times, when creating the lightbulb, he only succeeded once, that was all he needed, one win, which outshined all of his past failures.

Success is achievable in any goal you pursue, the only time success will never be obtained, is when the pursuer, gives up on achieving the goal. So, pick yourself up, every time, dust yourself off, and give it another try, until you succeed.

How To Achieve Anything

Be Disciplinely Persistent and Persistently Disciplined.

A bold topic, and let me warn you this is a very simple formula, however, it requires hard work but you are on a worthwhile journey to a better life, so strap in and let's go. There are only three steps to achieving anything you desire most in life, here they are:

1. Write down clearly, the major desire you want from your life.
2. Identify clear, precisely what you intend to give to achieve this desire
3. Begin giving right now. Receiving will follow.

The Desire

Everything that exists started with a desire, someone thought about it, for whatever reason and it was such an intense pull they just had to explore creating it into existence, from, aeroplanes, cars, buildings, bridges, teacups, lightbulbs, Google, Facebook, Netflix. Even this book you are reading, I had the desire to write it for you, weeks before I even wrote a word.

The desire you cannot shake, which calls and challenges you to achieve it - it must be pursued. Yes, you do not have the skills or knowledge to achieve it but you have been tapped by the unmistaken force of nature to embark on this journey. Nature will not allow you to rest peacefully until you deliver or at least attempt, it's calling.

A great desire holds the power to erect, a passionate, strong, uncontestable drive to accomplish tasks that you had no interest in the day before. My thirtieth birthday was my ultimate desire, push or calling, to change my downward spiralling life. I had no plan, no way of knowing how I would achieve anything but I knew this, I was going to do anything until I succeed, and I would succeed no matter what.

Look at your life now, who are the people and the things you have and enjoy the most. Think back to a time before you had these things in your life or that special someone, even your children, they were once just distant dreams, how did you feel? Think about when you were on track to achieve these great things you now cherish? How excited and focus you got. You wanted it, you had to have it and nothing was going to stand in your way. That is the force of desire, to pursue a goal with discipline and persistence until it is achieved.

The Cost

Everything comes at a cost, nothing is free. Your desires will cost you something, what you agree to pay will determine how serious you are and how much you will receive in return. For you to live the unlimited, fulfilled, happy, successful life of freedom you desire, will cost you a few things, such as:

1. Time watching pointless TV and browsing social media.
2. Time spent in the company of gossiping unmotivated friends.
3. Time away from negative relatives.
4. Time not stuck in a job you do not like, doing what you do not want.
5. Time spent in regret.

These are just a few but you get it, and I hope you agree that these are prices worth paying. Look, you are already spending the time, the 24 hours you are awarded each day will run out, the day does not care what you do with it, when it is finished, it is finished. Only you can determine what you use your time to do, you are already spending the time just start spending it more wisely.

The Plan

Get started, it is the most important part. I don't mean start by putting up the roof, that's the wrong way to build a house. I mean, you should write it down, commit your desires to paper, design a plan, bring your desire out of your mind and into reality - make it real. Again, the great buildings, products and services you see and use every day were all designed on paper before being physically created.

Spend quality time in the planning stage of your goals, Map Out your entire goal on paper, create a complete blueprint of the mechanics of your goals. You will be able to see what works well, what needs improving and what will not work the way you imagined it. Your planning stage is a fluid process, so make the changes needed to best help you achieve your overall goals.

Let's take an overview look at the skills required for efficient planning. The more effectively you can apply these skills, the better your plan and the better your end result will be.

Break It Down and Reverse Engineer.

Reverse engineering your goals is a worthy skill for anyone to have, and it is a simple skill to master. It is the application of small and medium-term milestones to achieve on the journey to your overall long-term desired goal. While it might seem sensible to approach a task by asking what do I need to do on the first day, then the second day, then the third day, and so on. I assure you, approaching any long-term plan in reverse is more effective, focusing on the desired end goal gives you better clarity when putting a plan together, which makes the planning stage more effective.

Let me show you, imagine you are about to build your dream house from the ground up. Right now, what is the first thing you see?... Your dream house, right. You can picture the house finished in all its magnificence in your head. Then you would now think about when you would like to complete it by, then, where ideally you want to build it, and then, how much it would cost and how you would fund it, then, when would you be able to start building your dream house.

You are able to see the end results before you start, visualisation is an incredible driver when you can, see, taste and feel your goal from the start.

Pursuing long-term desires can become overwhelming, many people simply get intimidated and give up before they can gain any traction. I suggest you practice the art of breaking down big goals into smaller pieces, a one-year goal plan can be broken into two 6 months goal plans. The six months goal plan broken into two quarterly goal plans, and then, broken down into monthly goal plans and then weekly, daily... you get the idea. Successfully complete each piece of tasks daily and at the end of the year, you should complete that massive once intimidating goal you started out to conquer.

Seek The Tools and Resource Needed.

You now know where you want to be at the end of your goal and at key stages of your master plan. A careful analysis of your plan will tell you what tools and resources you will require in order to achieve your goals. This will enable you to plan effectively and give you the best chances of achieving your end goals.

Tools and resources can be physical, software and also humans, in the form of knowledge and skills they bring to help accomplish the goal. By now I hope we have established that you are an extraordinary person, special and capable of anything you put your mind to. However, no man or woman is an island and that goes for the creation of your masterplan, the bigger your goals the more brains will be required to help you best accomplish them. Leverage the partnership of others, to assist in your mission, by creating a mastermind group of people will be your most effective path to success.

Taking Action Is Your Only Real Job

You will never always be motivated,
So you must learn to be disciplined.
-Unknown-

The athlete can only cross the finish line, if she first gets off the start line. Preparation is a key component to achieving success but taking action is the only way to actually succeed. But, she wants to pursue her goal, she is determined to accomplish it and she planned it all out masterfully, why would she not take action?

We all want to aspire to be our best in life and everything we do. No one wakes up thinking I will work very hard to be a subfraction of what I can really achieve, I want to be less than I really am. We all want to achieve all we can. 100% of us want to do well but only 2% gets to, the other 98% get caught out by resistance, we will dig into this further on the topic of Battling Resistance.

Taking action simply means, getting up and following the plan you have designed, only take the actions which will directly enable you to meet the goals you are working towards. The two underlying tools used to accomplish any goals are Discipline and Persistence.

You are not choosing to live less than you are right now, you are not choosing to let your dreams die, you are not choosing to let the life experiences and incredible successes you could truly achieve go un-experienced by you. No, you are not, but you are choosing not to be disciplined and persistence in achieving your goals. If you learn to master these two tools to work in your favour, you will not believe how amazing a life you will live.

Today, 98% of people are disciplined in not taking the right actions needed to change their lives. They are persistently putting things off till later or tomorrow or next year or after they get a promotion, their discipline and persistence have been hijacked by resistance. The sad thing is they think they are in control of their own lives, not knowing they are the captain asleep at the wheel of their ship - drifting to wherever life takes them.

Taking action also requires you to know what actions not to take, what to pay attention to and what to discard. So, how do you know what actions not to take, what to discard, how not to spend your time? This is simply, any action that will not directly or indirectly lead you to achieve the overall life goals you are pursuing. Remember, anything that is not driving you to accomplish your life goals are not worth your time or attention. You do not have to do everything under the sun, to live an accomplished, successful and prosperous life.

Always be driving all decisions, efforts, actions and thoughts in the direction of your life goal, to do anything else is an unproductive activity.

Discipline and Persistence.

Procrastination is the enemy, the silent assassin to your goals. You should stand guard at the door of your goals, armed and ready to fight procrastination, fight hard and fight with pride, passion and honour.

There are two fundamental weapons to defeat procrastination, Discipline and Persistence. Discipline, an Art to be mastered, it requires resisting the multitudes of distractions trying to stop you from your accomplishments.

Persistence is a Science, it is a universal law, that repetition will result in improvement, which breaths success. Discipline and Persistence are Siamese Twins, separate them and neither will function on its own.

You are either disciplined or you are not. You are either persistent or not. You cannot be a bit, or a certain percentage of either, this is an all or nothing quality. Because everything you do affects everything else you do, you will not succeed in being disciplined in one area of life and not in another. Same goes for persistence, you either are or you are not. Now, these are not skills accomplished overnight but be determined and work to develop them over your lifetime and they will richly reward you in return.

98% of people are not disciplined or persistent, hence their lifestyle and level of accomplishments. They live an unsatisfying life which they constantly pray would be better, if only they knew, all it takes is a change of attitude and the way they do the little things.

You now have the secrets to achieve success and the tools to fight failure. During the planning stages of all your tasks, implement methods to overcome procrastination, you will not see them all ahead of time but you should put guards at the ready, for when they appear. Create routine systems and checkpoints to ensure your plan is always moving forward and fulfilling its highest potentials. The best I have for you is to keep on working.

Enthusiasm

Enthusiasm is a positive mental attitude, you should express yourself with enthusiasm. Deliver your message with energy and enthusiasm in order to influence others.

Put enthusiasm into all that you do, from speaking to a handshake. Pray with enthusiasm. It is an infectious attitude, the people around you and everyone you communicate with should see and feel your level of energy, passion and commitment to your association with them. If you are a car salesperson, attempting to tell a potential buyer about the great features, quality and positive safety benefits of a car, you have to pitch them with such enthusiasm that they can feel every word and picture clearly every description you convey to them.

Whatever you do and truly believe in, put everything you have into it, the way you feel inside should shine outwards in all your representations.

Do not try to fake enthusiasm, it should be authentic, find the good points that excite you about the topic or thing which you want to convey to others.

Here are a few enthusiasm points to focus on when you want someone else to get excited about what you want to tell them.

When meeting people

1. Turn on your enthusiasm.
2. Greet them with a firm handshake.
3. Direct the conversation to focus on the person.
4. Ask questions which keep the focus on the person.

Since you have shown them so much care and attention, they are inclined to return the favour and not only listen attentively to you when it is your turn to speak but also clear their mind to feel every word you tell them.

Evolve Thinking, Make The Game Winnable

Impossible Is Something That Has Not Been Achieved, Yet.

This topic will be a broad-brush description, as there is an unlimited number of approaches to a problem, based on the many variables in play. When approaching any problem, I first start with the desired solution I am pursuing. Note, a solution is a solution but it might not be the best that is available, so, ensure you dive deeper to extract the very best solution you can.

When you work in the future, as we have established earlier, all solutions should be aimed at solving the long-term problem. Let's use a business example, you open a small-town restaurant, what is your purpose? To serve people food... Well, that is one way to approach it.

I would say 'To serve the community for years to come, to create a comforting place where families and friends can create and share life experiences'. Why this outlook? Because you are thinking about the long-term purpose of the business and the relationships and service you want to create for your customers, long-term. Fast forwards twenty years into the future, many local people will remember their experiences in your restaurant, the marriage proposals, first dates, first job, key business lunches, winning the annual pie-eating contest. Evolve thinking looks ahead in time and creates for it.

Working backwards, analysis and anticipate all the possible obstacles you might face, whilst implementing your solutions. Any new solutions will be a new process into your life or business, and there might be other variables at play which will be affected and/or might affect your new future process. Solutions must also be future proof, frequently brainstorming new ideas to solve the same problems over and over again is a stagnant process, not a wise use of time and resources. Remember a solution is a solution but not necessarily the best one, so fine the best solution to completely solve the problem and move on to the next.

Evolve thinking requires you to think and see in the future, in three dimensions. To take the problem and play it forward, then take the solution and play it forward, projecting its lifecycle and how it should work once implemented, what other elements, processes, people, will it interact with and how. What affects, should it have on them, can they be measured to determine its level of success?

Evolve thinking is not putting a plaster on a cut and waiting for it to heal. It is the cells that work to fight off infections and heal the cut, keeping the living organism alive and healthy to carry on stronger than before.

Extra Mile Principles, Stretch, Play, Live Beyond The Masses

A man who refuses to do more than he is paid for,
will seldomly be paid for more than he is doing.
-Earl Nightingale-

There are three ways to do something, the wrong way, the right way and better than anyone expected, even you (Extra Mile Baby!). Going above and beyond might seem uneconomical for many people because you will not earn any additional financial payment for the extra mile you put in, you still get paid the same as the others who just did exactly what was requested.

Whiles going the extra mile will benefit your clients with more than they paid for, it will also benefit you with new skills and abilities to do more than you could previously. Remember, greatness is on the top shelf, so keep reaching higher, you will be able to tap into a new level of quality, service and ability to execute. Always think of going the extra mile as a challenge to push yourself and what you believe you can achieve further with each task. Strive to engage more intimately with the next client, to listen, learn, understand and cater for them more than the last client and keep repeating this challenge indefinitely. This becomes another snowball effect development, you just keep getting stronger and better at what you do.

There are many ways a waiter can deliver a sandwich to a customer. With a pleasant smile, a recommendation of sauce the customer should eat the sandwich with, to give it that extra buzz or just wishing they enjoy their sandwich before he walks away. It's just a sandwich, Yes, but the way the customers are served adds to the overall enjoyment of the sandwich and their overall dining experience.

Your customers should be getting more value, benefits and maximum advantage from their interactions with you. This is a win for the customers and a bigger win for you, the more they get the more they will require from you and the more likely they will recommend your service to others. So, pure it on when your customers come around, give them the royal treatment, put them at the centre of your universe, each and every time and let them feel it through every interaction. Let them not want to leave your side, and most likely they will not. The aim is to create a lifetime relationship with them.

Leading Others To Take Massive Action

As we look ahead into the next century,
leaders will be those who empower others.
-Bill Gates-

Your team should already know your story, your vision, your mission, why you feel you are the right person to take on this calling life pitched you. Leadership is not about pushing or pulling others into action. There are various leadership types and strategies, I will give you the foundations of leadership, in my humble opinion.

Leaders, give their team apart of their own vision to care for, nurture and guide to success. In my own vision to *Help People Live Better Lives*, when recruiting team members, I show them my vision and then show them how their own skills and passionate contributions, as a member of my team, will help to achieve the overall goal but most importantly how their contributions will help fulfil their own purpose, their own goals in life and the lives of the people they will help.

This then makes it not only them working on my mission to achieve my goals but they are also working on their own mission to achieve their own personal goals, and contributing to improving someone else's life. This gives everyone pride, purpose and fulfilment in their work, you not only get long-term team members but also ones pushing to bring the most value to your mission and pulling clients to you. They become their own driven ecosystem, and you do not have to reignite them over and over with motivation.

Influence The World with your Message

Focus on your customers, not your competitors.
-Jeff Bazos-

Branding is important, however, branding is not the logo, company name nor the products and services you provide. Your brand is what you represent, believe in, it is who you are. Disney World is not a theme park, it is a family adventure world. Google is not a search engine, it is the window to the world of information.

What will you, your business, your product, be to your clients? They can get the products you offer from your competitors. It is not about the item you are selling, it is about the solution you are offering them like no one else can.

You run a small coffee stand outside a corporate office, you don't just sell them coffee, they can get that at home, from Starbucks or from the office coffee maker. You have to sell them something more, the energy to start their day, the pick-me-up to face their boss and deliver that key presentation. Your approach and presence are vital, do not just sell them coffee, they can buy that anywhere.

You influence your clients and the world by offering a solution to the problem they are facing. Remember, you do not have to dominate all corners of the market, you only have to dominate the segment of the market you chose to server. Focus on trying to solve your clients' problems, make them feel safe and open to come to you, knowing you have their best interest at heart and will do all you can to assist them. You never have to grab at their wallets, they will happily pay you what you ask, repeatedly if you can satisfy their needs.

Love your clients and want more for them than they want for themselves, then put all your actions into bringing them solutions, show them what you are doing for them. Let them see that you care and you are hard at work on their behalf. Become an irresistible force to them, give them no other option but to seek only you when they are in need.

Battling Resistance

Like Personal Development, this will be a life challenge and one you should stand guard against else it will rob you of meeting your full potentials. Resistance is the dark invisible force, which breaths procrastination and self-doubts, it is the storyteller who convinces you you are not good enough and your goals are not achievable. Resistance is a genius, a magician, a force of nature, it is the ultimate enemy of success which never sleeps, and you are its target. Think Star Wars, resistance is Darth Vader on the hunt to destroy.

We have established that 100% of people on the planet want to live up to their full potential, however, 98% of people do not live up to their full potential. So, why only 2% of the whole get to reach their universal desires? The answer is, the dark forces of resistance has captured the majority.

What are the 2% doing, that the 98% are not? The 2% are disciplined and persistent, they show up every day and put the work in, they push through adversity. The 2% club which anyone who wishes can become a member, get up off the sofa at 30 years old and look at their life and say 'No' this is not for me anymore, I will make a plan, I will seek the knowledge, I will do the work UNTIL I SUCCEED.

I cannot overemphasize this enough, success is not a secret. It is simply the mastery of discipline and persistence nothing more. To understand and learn to fight resistance I recommended you read '*The War Of Art by Steven Pressfield*' it will do you great justice and equip you to succeed.

Resistance is that nag you get when you should, or are about to do something challenging to better your life. It starts to pull and seduce you to indulge in short-term pleasures, which gives you no long-term benefits. Since you now know better, and you want to be apart of that elite 2% club, you can now tell resistance to be quiet, you are on your way to the big leagues.

Money Management, Secure Your Future

Just because you can afford something,
does not mean you should buy it.

Some people find this subject sensitive to discuss, I can't really tell why but I like the topic. We have been conditioned to work towards making money since we started school, everything we have been learning is tailored towards getting a job, which pays us money, so we can have money to spend. Even though you have been working towards the attainment of money from childhood, no one actually thought you how to manage it. Many people's little knowledge of money management revolves around three activities, they are, *Get It - Save It - Spend It.*

Whilst there is certainly nothing wrong with these three approaches, we all do them. Money management requires you to know when and how to best implement these actions. I recommend you read an amazing book *'The Richest Man In Babylon by George S. Clason'.* It lays out the basic formula of money management and wealth-building, boiled down so simple you cannot miss nor fail to master them with ease.

Everyone's personal situation is different, people have different incomes and expenses, however, I will tell you that does not matter in the science of money management. Money management requires a structured, disciplined, persistent plan. The rich people I know do not worry about money, not because they have an abundance of it, no, they do not have to worry about money because they manage it very well.

The formula for money management (The Richest Man In Babylon)

1. Secure a regular income
2. Save at least 10% of all income
3. Control your expenses
4. Invest your savings, for-profit
5. Protect your investments/saving from loss
6. Secure a future income
7. Increase your ability to earn more

This is a simple formula, that anyone with true wealth can attest to, as being an effective system to grow and manage wealth. Start now with what you have and when your fortune starts to grow, you will be amazed at the lifestyle you can create for yourself and your family and get rid of your money problems, for good.

Enterprise Building, Create Your Own Financial Ecosystem

Work on your business, not in your business.
-Michael E. Gerber-

The topic of enterprise building would take an entire book, I want to focus on personal development but this topic is worth exploring. You first have to become the person with, focus, mindset, principles, skills and confidence, in order to build and maintain a successful enterprise. If you apply what you have learnt in this book so far, you will become such a person ready to successfully create and lead an enterprise.

I know, not everyone wants to be a business owner, many greatly successful people live happy fulfilled lives as employees but building your own enterprise does not mean quitting your job and setting up your own shop. For example, Sheryl Sandberg, Facebook's COO, Tim Cook, Apple CEO, Jamie Dimon JP Morgan Chairman & CEO are all employees. Presidents and Prime Ministers, of democratic countries, are employees, they have a job. What they all have in terms of personal enterprises are income assets, such as rental properties, they own businesses, investments, stocks/bonds etc. You too can be an employee and still build yourself a fruitful enterprise on the side, I highly encourage you to do so.

For the hardcore entrepreneurs (employees can use these same systems) when building and managing a business, ensure you have a clear goal for the business' long-term mission and what you most desire for your clients, and give them more than they want for themselves.

Elements of a successful enterprise:

1. Solves problems
2. Operate on the Extra Mile Principles
3. Purpose and services are clear to understand by the team and clients
4. Operates on multiple sources of income
5. Have a strong, complementary backend business services
6. Is structure to keep clients long-term, by taking them on a lifetime journey
7. Implement multiple referral systems
8. Have a passionate, evolve thinking management

This is my passion and area of expertise, I wish you the very best in building your enterprise. I wish to see you strive and be successful and if there is anything I can do to assist your mission, reach out to me.

Your Own Passive Income System

The ultimate financial point of creating your own enterprise (Entrepreneurs or Employees) is to create a system which generates and sustains passive income for you.

Passive income is when you continue to get paid after the work is done. This includes royalties from books, movies, or songs and also revenues that comes from real estate or business investments, where you do not have to be present to earn it.

This sounds amazing, it is a simple system. These principles should be applied along with the formula from the Money Management Secure Your FutureTopic. For a deep dive into this topic, I recommend you read '*Rich Dad Poor Dad's Cashflow Quadrant by Robert T. Kiyosaki'*.

The only two ways, *that I know of*, to create great amounts of passive income and wealth are to become a Business Owner and An Investor.

A business owner owns the business, *not work for it*. A shop owner who cannot leave his business else it will fall apart is not a business owner, the business owns him, his time and efforts are needed to keep the business running. He cannot go on holiday for too long and not worry about the business falling apart.

Be an owner and an investor. You are free to work on the overall vision and direction of your business or simply just invest in the business, without any responsibility for the daily business activities. Both approaches, of course, require you to seek the knowledge and advice of credible experts before you part with your money. When investing in or going into business I would highly recommend you do so with something you understand, not necessarily in minute detail but enough to make a confident assessment.

My first major business was the investment company, Live Free Investment, which I still own. It has holdings in 15 different companies all over the world, none of which I play any part in running, I am just an investor, who put my money at work in those companies and I get profits in return.

Getting The Best Out Of You

Make Better Decisions, Get Better Results.
-Dwayne 'The Rock' Johnson-

We have established that the decisions we make determine the outcomes of our lives, and since we then have to live with those decisions, wouldn't it be great if we learn how to make the best decisions, to begin with... Better Decisions = Better Life.

Below I've listed a few everyday decision categories you will face and I believe if you follow them you will start to build a strong armour of disciplines and persistence.

Ethics

Do not give half a day's work for a full day's pay. Any actions you take should be ethical, both to yourself and others, even if they would not have known otherwise. Do not allow yourself to do things which you are not proud to sing from the mountains for all to hear.

Wealth

True wealth is not the vast amount of money or material things you possess, it is the people you love who share their life experiences with you. Take stock of how wealthy you truly already are and embrace them. Everything else is just extra stuff.

Working and Relaxing.

If you have to split your day into two activities - Work and Relax, always do the Work first and Relax after, you will enjoy and appreciate your time to relax more knowing you have completed your work.

Completing Assignments

Set Goals. Write a plan, starting with the desired outcome first - you will be better equipped to complete your assignment when you have a clearly laid out blueprint road map to follow.

Productive Conversations

Before you make an important phone call or enter a meeting. Write down the topics you wish to address and the desired outcomes you want. Nothing is more unprofessional than, "Sorry, I forgot what I wanted to say".

Measuring Interaction Success

Before every important interaction (and all interactions should be important), write down your goals for the interaction. Knowing your desired outcomes, you can then review your notes to ensure you achieved your goals before moving on.

Comparing Choices

When choosing between two or more choices, choose the one which will challenge you to give more of yourself and resources to help others. If you are thinking to tip a valet, $10 or $20 for a service you felt was amazing, give the $20 tip, you will feel better that you gave the most you wanted to give, you will not feel as if you shortchanged the amazing service you received and you will make the valet's day $10 happier. Always, give more, do more, extra mile baby.

Recording Information

Don't trust your memory. You might have figured out by now, that I am a big fan of writing things down. Taking notes on the go should be apart of our daily activities. Have you ever had an idea or thought you felt was amazing? It just caught you off guard, it was inspiring, then later when you try to recall it, you cannot remember. Keep a notebook or note-taking app, to record inspirational thoughts and ideas which might later become valuable gold to you. Do not leave important things in your head, they have a way of escaping.

Quality vs Quantity

It is not how many hours you put in, it is what you put into the hours.

The man is going, he is at it 24/7, 365, boy does he work hard, he sure puts in a lot of time, yet his results do not reflect his input. Measure your input versus your results. Input is an investment, the output should be paid back with dividends.

Feed Your Brain The Right Stuff

What you put in, you get out with multiples. If you put rubbish in your brain, you will get a rubbish life multiplied your input. I recommend you become a good student, not a follower, a student. Learn the things to do and learn the things not to do, to reach your goals. Read the right books, learn from the right mentors, study the right courses. Stand guard at the gates of your mind, at all times, keep the rubbish out.

Thoughts

What you think about manifests into your reality. Fill your mind with positive, creative accomplishing thoughts. If you wish to live a happy successful life, it starts with the thoughts you allow and keep playing in your mind. Keep your mind clear of unproductive, time-wasting negative thoughts, leave it free to work on the positive, creative, productive, happiness you want to bring and enjoy into your physical life.

Start The Day Right

Start your day with gratitude, be thankful. Start your day by successfully completing a small task and acknowledge the small success. This puts your brain in an accomplished mood, that it will want to feed on through the day, so it will be more enthusiastic to complete the next tasks and then the next. Plan your day out on paper the night before and imaging you completing each task. Get into your day with a positive attitude, feeling like you have already completed all the tasks to come.

Evolving To The Next Level, Mastery

If you don't like how things are,
change it! You're not a tree.
-Jim Rohn-

Even as an employee, do not wait to be given a raise, instead, start performing at the level of the higher position job you are after. Ensure your boss sees that you are ready and worthy of that higher position and all the benefits that come with it. Take the initiative, ask your boss to let you work in the higher position you are after at your current pay rate for 30-90 days. If at the end of the agreed period they feel you are not qualified, you will remain in your current role till you are, otherwise, you should be promoted to the higher position with the higher pay rate. What is the worst that could happen? You gain extra experiences, skills, confidence and qualities you did not have before. You can stay and wait for the promotion or take your new-found skills and move on to another company who sees your higher value.

Two types of people that amount to nothing:
1. Those who cannot do as they are told.
2. Those who do nothing else.

Those who amount to anything in life are those who move on their own personal initiatives, without being told what to do or why they should do it. A winner never quits and a quitter never wins.

When you reach a new level of Extra Mile living, celebrate, you deserve it, then set new goals to move to the next level. Growth never stops, there is always more you can do, more you can achieve, more and other ways you can help people.

Do not become stagnant, one without goals to drive them forward is like a rock, it has no use for itself, it just sits there waiting to be picked up and put into action at someone else's command. Pay greate attention to the person you are, and ensure that person is exactly who you want to be or is aspiring to become. Do not live a life you did not design for yourself, do not live a life you are not in complete undeniable control of.

You are now armed with the fundamental tools to, Become The Person You Most Admire. Think Extra Mile, give Extra Mile service, seek Extra Mile results for your clients and live an Extra Mile life for yourself. This is now your new level of life, you are not a competitor, you are what others aspire to become, you are the standard by which true greatness is measured. If you are not there yet, what an incredible goal to set for yourself and the remarkable things you will discover about yourself on your journey to become.

Look up and around you, as far as the eyes can see,
there is no roof, there are no walls, life gave you no limits.
-Miguel Williams-

Recommended Books to Read

The Richest Man In Babylon - George Clason
The War Of Art - Steven Pressfield
Getting Everything You Can Out Of All You've Got - Jay Abraham
Think And Grow Rich - Napoleon Hill
Principles Life and Work - Ray Dalio
The Moment Of Lift - Melinda Gates
Rich Dad's Cashflow Quadrant - Robert T. Kiyosaki
Play Bigger - Al Ramadam, Dave Peterson,
Christopher Lochhead, Kevin Maney
7 Strategies for Wealth & Happiness - Jim Rohn

**For success in life and in business,
I recommend that you study the philosophies of:**

Warren Buffet - Jim Rohn - Russel Branson
Grant Cardone - Moya Greene - Jay Abraham - Ray Dalio
Tony Robbins - Sheryl Sandberg - Charlie Munger - Jeff Bezos

Become

How to be the person you most admire

MIGUEL WILLIAMS